Ban Seng Hoe # Timeless
Splendour

Treasures from the National Museum of China

Published by the Canadian Museum of Civilization Corporation (CMCC)
100 Laurier Street, P.O. Box 3100, Station B
Gatineau, Quebec J8X 4H2

Manager, Publishing: Deborah Brownrigg
Coordinator, Publishing: Ginette L. Côté
Graphic Design: Teixeira Design
Photography: National Museum of China
Printer: Tri-Graphic Printing

Library and Archives Canada
Cataloguing in Publication
Hoe, Ban Seng, 1939-
Timeless Splendour: treasures from the
National Museum of China / Ban Seng Hoe.

Souvenir booklet from the exhibition Treasures from China, at the Canadian Museum of Civilization, May 11 to October 28, 2007.
Issued also in French under title: Splendeurs du temps, trésors du Musée national de Chine.
ISBN 978-0-660-19704-3
Cat. no.: NM24-17/2007E

1. Art, Chinese—Exhibitions.
2. China—Antiquities—Exhibitions.
3. China—Civilization—Exhibitions.
4. Zhongguo guo jia bo wu guan—Exhibitions.
I. Canadian Museum of Civilization.

N7343.5.H63 2007   709.51074'714221   C2007-980042-4

Front cover image:

Horse and Trainer
Tang Dynasty (A.D. 618–907)
Horse height: 40 cm / Trainer height: 36.8 cm
These burial objects depict a tug-of-war between horse and trainer, in which the sturdy horse appears reluctant to obey its trainer. The trainer's muscles show his strength; his face shows his determination to lead the lively animal. The horse is equipped with a saddle, a cushion and a string of small round bells on its back.

Back cover images, left to right:

Famille Rose Vase
Daoguang Period (A.D. 1821–1850), Qing Dynasty
Height: 32 cm / Body diameter: 18 cm / Base diameter: 10.5 cm
On this vase, a lively egret searches for food against a background of red lotus flowers and lush green leaves. The egret and lotus together symbolize success in passing civil examinations and promotion to higher positions. The six seal script characters on the base say "Made in the Year of Daoguang of Great Qing."

Zisha Teapot
Ming Dynasty (A.D. 1368–1644)
Height: 10 cm / Length: 19.3 cm / Width: 12 cm
Zisha is a special kind of clay from Yixing, Jiangsu Province. It has a relatively high iron content and its fine texture does not require glaze. Its usual colours are brown, light yellow and dark purple. The exterior of this pot resembles the bark of an ancient tree and expresses a classical simplicity. It was made by a famous folk artist of the Ming Dynasty, Gong Chun, a servant who accompanied his master to studies in a Buddhist temple and learned ceramics from the monks.

Flowerpot from the Jun Kiln
Song Dynasty (A.D. 960–1279)
Height: 23 cm / Rim diameter: 23.4 cm / Base diameter: 14 cm
It was once said that the price of gold is high, but Jun ware is priceless. The Jun kiln was in today's Yu County, Henan Province. This elegant pot was used either as a jardinière or as a decorative item. Its unusual colour comes from the oxidization of copper in the glaze during firing. The bottom of the pot features the Chinese character for "three", and has five holes, presumably for draining water.

Foreword

This book, and the exhibition it complements, are the rewards of a partnership forged between our two national museums in 2003. That partnership is based on our common interest in human history, our commitment to cultural exploration, and our shared belief in the importance of understanding and dialogue among all peoples.

Treasures from China offers Canadians a unique insight into 4,000 years of Chinese history and cultural development. As the book and the exhibition reveal, China's journey from ancient times to the modern era has been long, tumultuous, and fascinating.

The exhibition features 120 artifacts from the National Museum of China. This book narrows the focus to 32. They include some of the most precious objects housed in the Chinese museum. Collectively, these treasures express China's rich and diverse cultural traditions, and confirm the mastery of its finest artists. Although the objects featured in this book are distinctly Chinese, they are also part of the common heritage of all humanity. We can all take pleasure in their beauty.

The museum exhibition surveys the grand sweep of Chinese history from the dawn of civilization to the end of the Imperial dynasties in 1911. But the book and exhibition also help us understand contemporary Chinese culture, and they may offer clues about China's cultural future.

Treasures from China was developed exclusively for the Canadian Museum of Civilization (CMC). In return, the CMC is developing an exhibition featuring the treasures of Canada's Aboriginal peoples, to be presented in collaboration with the National Museum of China in Beijing when that city hosts the Olympic Games in 2008.

The agreement that set the stage for this cultural exchange was signed in Beijing's Great Hall of the People in the presence of the Prime Minister of Canada and the Premier of the People's Republic of China. Both governments saw the exchange as a gesture of friendship between our two countries, and as a means of promoting mutual understanding. On behalf of our museums and our visitors, we endorse those thoughts and we look forward to more collaboration in the years to come.

Lu Zhangshen
Director
National Museum of China

Victor Rabinovitch
President and CEO
Canadian Museum of Civilization

Boat-Shaped Pot
Yangshao Culture
Neolithic Period
(ca. 5000–3000 B.C.)
Excavated at Baoji,
Shaanxi Province, 1958
Height: 16 cm
Length: 23.5 cm

This vessel was used to draw water. The black fishnet design on the body suggests that the Neolithic Chinese were already using nets to catch fish, while also using the motif as a decorative pattern.

Preface

We represent different countries, but we share a common experience: as diplomats, we grew up in one culture and were later immersed in another. The experience is wonderfully enriching. For Canadians, **Treasures from China** might not offer a full cultural immersion, but it does represent a fine first step.

To understand today's China, one must understand the country's past. That is no easy feat. China's archaeological record reaches back a million years. Its political history is among the longest, most complex, and most colourful on the planet. Its contributions to human civilization, and to the world's material culture, have been extraordinary.

Most people who read this book or attend the exhibition will likely be drawn to those things that distinguish Chinese culture from their own. This is, after all, an opportunity to learn about a distant land, and about people with an unfamiliar history and heritage; however, we should not overlook the many attributes that our countries have in common.

Canada and the People's Republic of China are both culturally diverse. Both have been enriched by the contributions of indigenous peoples and others who came from afar. Both have benefitted enormously from cultural and commercial interactions with the outside world, including interactions with each other. Both have been blessed by nature but are defined, to a large extent, by geography. Both countries have entered the twenty-first century with confidence and determination to build a better future.

It is also true that Canadian and Chinese people are curious about each other. They want to better understand their neighbours across the Pacific, especially in these times of globalization. **Treasures from China**, and the reciprocal exhibition on Canada's Aboriginal peoples, will help satisfy that curiosity. They will help promote mutual understanding and respect. For that, we express our appreciation to the National Museum of China and the Canadian Museum of Civilization.

The Canadian and Chinese peoples have at least one other thing in common: an appreciation for creative genius, whatever its nationality, whatever its vintage, whatever its form. Above all else, **Treasures from China** is a celebration of creative genius. We hope it is a catalyst for further study and cultural exchange.

Lu Shumin
Ambassador of the
People's Republic of
China to Canada

Joseph Caron
Ambassador of Canada to Japan
(Former Ambassador of Canada to
the People's Republic of China)

Black Pottery Goblet
Shangdong Longshan Culture
Late Neolithic Period
(ca. 2500–2000 B.C.)
Excavated at Jiaoxian,
Shandong Province, 1975
Height: 13 cm
Rim diameter: 14.5 cm
Base diameter: 6.3 cm

This type of pottery is particularly thin, and is known as "eggshell pottery". The stem and body were made separately, then fitted together. The black colour resulted from the use of charcoal during the first firing. Wet firewood was added to the kiln at a relatively low temperature, with the carbon from the resulting smoke permeating the pottery, turning it black.

Introduction

The great Yangtzi and Yellow Rivers appear on a map of China as long, undulating lines that run parallel to each at both ends, but swing dramatically in opposite directions in the middle, coursing up and down the map like mirror images. The rivers are a useful metaphor for the country's history. It has also experienced ups and downs, unity and disunity. But like the long lines of its two great rivers, the central thread of Chinese civilization remains unbroken.

Despite a succession of dynasties, mainstream Chinese culture has always managed to adapt and change. Internally, it has integrated and accommodated diverse ethnic cultures, which have contributed to ongoing regeneration and a vibrant tradition of unity in diversity. Externally, China has absorbed countless foreign influences and ideas, adding to the richness and complexity of its own society.

The internal influences include intercultural exchanges with more than 56 ethnic peoples, such as the Dang Xiang, the Xianbei, the Mongols and the Manchu. External influences have also been many and varied. They came from Central and Western Asia following the opening of the Silk Road; they came from Southeast Asia, Arabia and Africa during the maritime explorations of the Ming Dynasty (A.D. 1405–1421); they came from the West, brought by missionaries, explorers and commercial interests. Among the greatest external influences was the introduction of Buddhism from South Asia.

These internal and external forces have combined to propel and shape Chinese history, society and culture, creating one of the world's most distinctive living civilizations. Of course, China's interest in the outside world has waxed and waned over the centuries. Here again, however, the great rivers of central China provide a useful analogy. Despite their meanderings, the ultimate direction of their flow to the seas is clear. Over the long course of its history, China has participated in cultural and economic exchange so that it, and the world, have reaped many benefits.

The exhibition, **Treasures from China**, presented the story of China's history and culture through a chronological setting of artifacts selected by the National Museum of China. The exhibition included a wide range of materials and styles, and provided information on historical, social and cultural contexts. Special reference was made to aesthetics, designs, symbols, functions and techniques. Overall, the artifacts provided a glimpse into the remarkable history of Chinese civilization.

This booklet showcases a selection of objects drawn from the exhibition. These objects reflect not only imperial tastes and the luxurious lifestyles of the wealthy, but also—as some of our Chinese colleagues have pointed out—the ingenuity, vitality and wisdom of the Chinese people.

To understand the Chinese people, we must understand their past: their cultural values, their ways of life, their philosophies, ideals and world-view. How has Chinese culture lasted so long? What factors have contributed to its endurance and adaptation over thousands of years? How do the Chinese decipher and interpret their own history and culture? How do today's Chinese view themselves and their place in the world? How do they position themselves to contribute to the wider world—and how will the world interact with China, both now and the future?

These are some of the questions that we hope are inspired by this book, the exhibition and its splendid Chinese treasures.

Painted Basin
Yangshao Culture
Neolithic Period
(ca. 5000–3000 B.C.)
Excavated at Xi'an,
Shaanxi Province, 1955
Height: 17 cm
Rim diameter: 40 cm
Base diameter: 7 cm

This basin covered a "coffin urn", used in the burial of a child. It is painted with a human face, with a nose shaped like an upside-down "T", and fish near both ears. The face and fish designs were likely used by a shaman to communicate with the netherworld and to protect the soul of the dead child.

Water Jar
Yangshao Culture
Neolithic Period
(ca. 5000–3000 B.C.)
Excavated at Baoji,
Shaanxi Province, 1958
Height: 46 cm
Diameter at handles: 22.5 cm
Base diameter: 2 cm

This vessel was used to draw water from rivers and wells. Rope was threaded through its ring-shaped handles to lower the jar into the water. When the jar was empty, its centre of gravity caused it to tip forwards; when it was full, it returned to an upright position. It was built up of ropes of clay, after which its surface was smoothed out.

Bronze Battle Axe
Shang Dynasty
(1600–1046 B.C.)
Excavated at Yidu,
Shangdong Province, 1965
Length: 31.7 cm
Width: 35.8 cm
Thickness: 0.5–1 cm

Used for close combat, this axe was also a ritual object symbolizing power and military authority. It came from a tomb that likely belonged to a man of wealth and influence.

Bronze Cowrie Container

Western Han Dynasty
(206 B.C.–A.D. 8)
Excavated at Jinning,
Yunan Province, 1956
Height: 43.5 cm
Base diameter: 21.8 cm

Cowrie shells were a form of
currency in ancient times. Two
tigers decorate this container's
biconcave body; the top
features seven oxen. Cattle
and buffalo are symbols of
wealth and influence in an
agricultural society, and the
tomb owner might have been
a man of high social status.
Made by the Dian people of
Yunan, this container suggests
exchange between bronze
cultures of the Central Plain
and southwestern China.

**Bronze *Zun*
(Wine Storage Vessel)**
Shang Dynasty
(1600–1046 B.C.)
Excavated at Funan,
Anhui Province, 1957
Height: 51 cm
Mouth diameter: 44.9 cm

There are three dragons on
the shoulder of this vessel,
and three tigers in relief
on the upper belly. The
complex ornamentation
indicates a high level of
bronze-casting technique.

**Bronze *Zun*
(Wine Storage Vessel)**
Eastern Zhou Dynasty
Spring and Autumn Period
(770–476 B.C.)
Excavated at Sanmenxia,
Henan Province, 1956
Height: 29 cm
Length: 31.5 cm

A cloud pattern decorates the
surface of this vessel, which
is shaped like an animal with
upright ears, short legs and a
short tail. A "*dou*-type" cup on
the back serves as an opening.

People of the Shang Dynasty believed in consulting their ancestors before any important event. This is a tortoise shell bearing oracle inscriptions. Rounded grooves were drilled into the back of the shell, with smaller holes chiselled alongside.

Oracle Tortoise Shell (Front View)
Shang Dynasty
(1600–1046 B.C.)
Length: 18.9 cm
Width: 10.2 cm

Heated metal was then burned into the grooves and holes, causing the shell to crack. The diviner made his predictions after reading the crackle lines on the front of the shells. The script in this shell predicts favourable circumstances.

Oracle Tortoise Shell
(Back View)
Shang Dynasty
(1600–1046 B.C.)
Length: 18.9 cm
Width: 10.2 cm

Fragments of Xiping Stone Classics

Eastern Han Dynasty
(A.D. 25–220)
Longest side: 47 cm
Thickness: 16 cm

During the Xiping Period
(A.D. 172–178) of the Eastern
Han Dynasty, the Confucian
classics were carved on stone
and erected in front of the
Imperial College at the capital
of Loyang. The classics are
the *Book of Songs*, the *Book of
History*, the *Book of Changes*,
the *Book of Rites*, the *Spring
and Autumn Annals*, the *Analects*
and the commentary of Gong
Yang. These stone documents
were produced to help settle
disputes, and to help interpret
Confucian classics following
the burning of the original
documents by the Qin Dynasty's
First Emperor, who wanted to
control political thought and
ideology. Due to war and neglect,
the stone classics were eventu-
ally broken up and scattered.

Bronze *Zhou Jie* (Shipping Pass) with Gold Inlay
Warring States Period (475–221 B.C.)
Excavated at Shou County, Anhui Province, 1957
Height: 30.9 cm
Width: 7.1 cm
Thickness: 0.6 cm

This bronze tally, issued by the King of Chu, provides Prince Qi, the Lord of E Prefecture, with a permit for water transportation. Such permits normally consisted of a section of bamboo, cut into two parts. Each party kept one of the sections. If the two halves fit perfectly, the permit was considered authentic. Permits specified the kind and quantity of goods to be carried, tax exemptions, and the tariff to be paid. They were reserved for the royal and aristocratic classes.

Landscape Painting by Wen Boren

Ming Dynasty
(A.D. 1368–1644)
Painting:
165.2 cm (L) x 40.2 cm (W)

Wen Boren, a nephew of the famous painter Wen Cheng-ming, was born in Wuxian, Jiangsu Province. This paper scroll records his tour of scenic places, depicting mountain peaks, dense forest, a cottage and a winding mountain road. His use of ink is carefully balanced between dark and light. The painting bears two seals with the artist's given name and his chosen pen name.

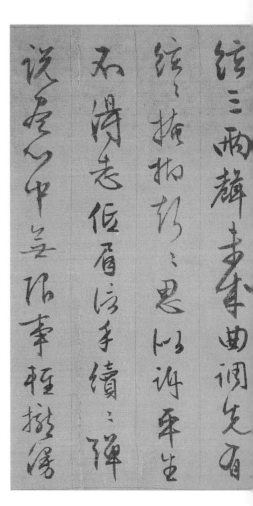

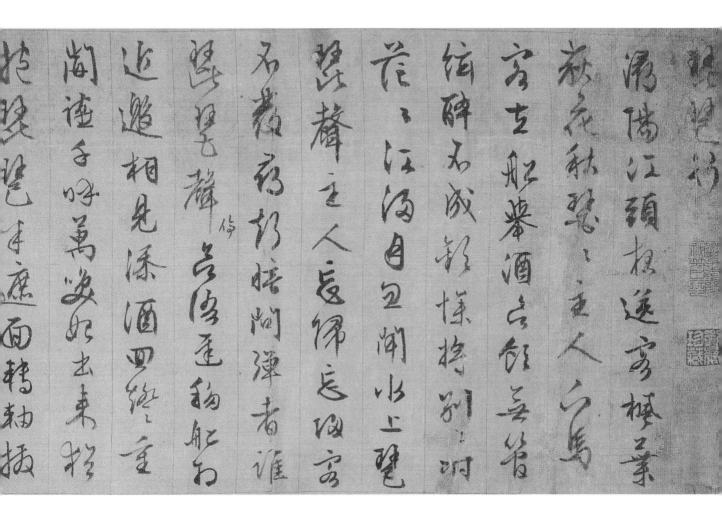

"Pi Pa Xing" in Running Script by Wen Zhengming
Ming Dynasty
(A.D. 1368–1644)
Height: 36 cm
Length: 250 cm

This poem was composed by renowned Tang Dynasty poet Bai Juyi, and was written on silk by Wen Zhengming during the Ming Dynasty. It describes a chance encounter on a boat, during which the artist was deeply moved by the music of a female entertainer on a *pi pa* (stringed instrument), and her stories of an unfortunate life. Wen was a specialist in all forms of calligraphy, but this running form shows his consummate skill. Two of the artist's seals are stamped at the right.

**Pictorial Brick
of Wine-Making**
Eastern Han Dynasty
(A.D. 25–220)
Excavated at Pengshan,
Sichuan Province, 1954
Height: 28.4 cm
Width: 38.3 cm
Thickness: 7 cm

This brick depicts wine production. Wine-making was an important Han industry, and taverns and wine-making facilities were found in many towns and cities. At the centre of the picture, a man stirs the contents in a cauldron, as his assistant tends the fire. The bottom of the picture features a filtering stove with urns for the wine. Nearby, a man stands ready with a cart of wine for sale.

Pictorial Brick of Acrobats Performing at a Banquet
Eastern Han Dynasty
(A.D. 25–220).
Excavated at Chengdu,
Sichuan Province, 1954
Length: 46 cm, Width: 40 cm
Thickness: 6 cm
Weight: approx. 30 kg

This brick, from a tomb chamber, shows the deceased watching performances by musicians and acrobats. He wears a hat and long gown, and is accompanied by a female musician. Two male performers are juggling, while a woman performs a dance with long scarves, accompanied by a drummer. The empty table in the centre of the picture indicates that the performance began following a banquet.

Gilded Bronze Statue of Guanyin
Five Dynasties
(A.D. 916–1125)
Excavated at the Wanfo
Pagoda in Jinhua,
Zhejiang Province, 1958
Height: 53 cm

Pottery Figure of a Heavenly King
Tang Dynasty
(A.D. 618–907)
Excavated at Xi'an,
Shaanxi Province, 1956
Height: 97 cm
Base: 27 x 19 cm

This fierce-looking figure is a tomb guardian and a protector of Buddhist law and order. He wears a helmet, armour and leggings. His armour is decorated with dragons' heads, and the edges of his inner clothing are curled like lotus leaves. His foot rests on a struggling *yaksa*, a malevolent being. The pose vividly expresses the strength and might of this protector.

Guanyin is the goddess of mercy, coming to the rescue of those who call upon her. She sits on an "artificial mountain", resting her hand on her knee in a meditative pose. She is also known as "water-moon Guanyin". This concept originated with the Dharmalaksana sect at the end of the seventh century, implying that everything is void and empty, like the reflection of moonlight on water.

**Polychrome
"Wucai" Plate**
Kangxi Period
(A.D. 1662–1722)
Qing Dynasty
Height: 2 cm
Diameter: 25.2 cm

The bottom of this plate features six characters in standard script surrounded by a double circle, stating that it was "Made in the Year of Kangxi of Great Qing." The five red bats on the exterior stand for great blessings. On the inner mouth there are four Chinese characters in seal script representing boundless longevity. "Wucai" (five colours) refers to the five-colour overglaze decoration.

Globular Vase in Contrasting Colours
Yongzheng Period
(A.D. 1723–1735)
Qing Dynasty
Height: 52.2 cm
Body diameter: 39 cm
Base diameter: 16.5 cm

This style of decorative vase —blue and white patterns under the glaze, with painted overglaze colours—is known as "contending coloured ware". The body is covered with a concentric floral pattern with cloud and *ruyi* ("as you wish") motifs. Surging waves and mountains at the base symbolize long life and riches. The bottom features six characters in seal script, stating "Made in the Year of Yongzheng of Great Qing."

Cizhou Jar
Yuan Dynasty
(A.D. 1271–1368)
Discovered in the sea at Suizhong County,
Liaoning Province, 1995
Height: 31.5 cm
Rim diameter: 18.5 cm
Body diameter: 30.5 cm
Base diameter: 11.2 cm

Cizhou is in today's Ci county, Hebei Province. This simple, down-to-earth jar was intended for practical use. Decorated with an exaggerated dragon and phoenix, and auspicious symbols of peace and prosperity, it reflects the folk traditions of northern China.

Blue and White Flask
Xuade Period
(A.D. 1426–1435)
Ming Dynasty
Height: 46.5 cm
Rim diameter: 10 cm
Base diameter: 14.8 cm

This brilliantly-coloured decorative flask features a white dragon with raised claws leaping through surging waves and foam. The dragon symbolizes imperial power and prosperity. The neck of the flask is covered with curling grass and interlaced lotus flowers.

Black Glazed Jug with Rooster Head
Eastern Jin Dynasty
(A.D. 317–420)
Excavated at Zhenjiang,
Jiangsu Province, 1969
Height: 16 cm
Rim diameter: 7.6 cm
Base diameter: 10.3 cm

This jug stored wine or water.
String or sinew was tied through
the two small round holders at
the shoulder. The jug's shape,
with rooster head, appeared
during the Jin Dynasty.

Red Porcelain Vase from the Lang Kiln

Kangxi Period
(A.D. 1662–1722)
Qing Dynasty
Height: 49 cm
Base diameter: 14.6 cm

This vase is named for Lang Tingji, Governor of Jaingsu Province and manager of the famous Jingdezhen kiln. Its typical shape features a short neck and a broad shoulder, tapering to a slightly extended base. As the glaze melts and flows downwards, the red at the bottom of the vase becomes richer and redder. It was hard to produce a satisfactory piece, because the firing technique made it difficult to control the temperature. An old folk saying suggested that if you wanted to be poor, you should produce red Lang ware.

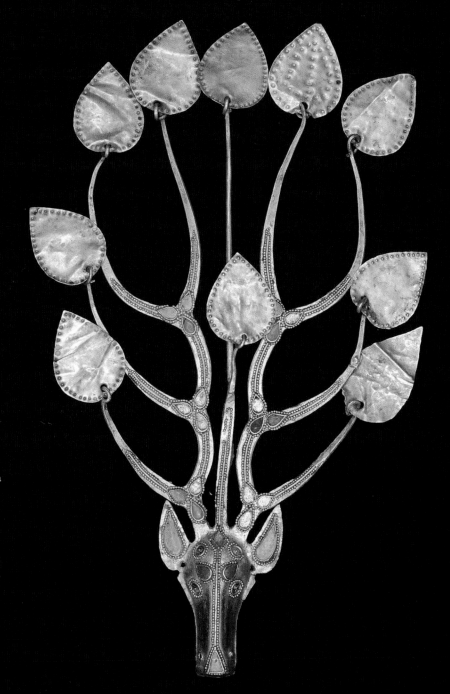

Gold Ornament Featuring Horse Head with Antlers

Northern Dynasties
(A.D. 386–581)
Excavated at Daerhan
Maoming'anqi,
Inner Mongolia, 1981
Height: 16.2 cm

This ornament was worn by a Xianbei aristocrat. The antlers on the horse's head have three branches with ten golden leaves. The leaves are attached with gold rings, causing them to sway when the wearer walks. This was known as *Bu Yao* ("moving with one's steps"). The animal decoration is believed to dispel evil and bring good fortune.

Round Golden Lacquer Box with Eight Immortals
Qing Dynasty
(A.D. 1644–1911)
Height: 7 cm
Diameter: approx. 24 cm

The eight Daoist immortals (six males and two females) appear frequently in art from the Ming and Qing periods. The immortals could make themselves invisible at will, and each possessed a different magical power, such as reviving the dead, curing the sick or helping the destitute. They also served as patron saints for florists, musicians and theatrical groups. On this superbly crafted box they are set in a landscape with gardens, mountains, stones, clouds, pine trees, weeping willows, high walls, rails and small bridges over the rivers.

**Red Lacquer Bowl
with Dragon and
Phoenix Designs**
Qianlong Period
(A.D. 1736–1795)
Qing Dynasty
Height: 7.2 cm
Rim diameter: 14.9 cm

This ornamental bowl features
the mark of the Qianlong
period on the bottom. The
dragon and phoenix motifs
are so minutely carved that
the scales and whiskers of the
dragon, and the feathers of
the phoenix, are visible. It is
said to have taken half a year
to complete the carving.

**Jade Censer with
Ring Handles**
Qing Dynasty
(A.D. 1644–1911)
Height: approx. 8 cm
Width: 16 cm

This drum-shaped jade piece
has ring handles, and is covered
with animal and cloud patterns,
as well as an ancient form of
the swastika, one of the auspicious signs in Buddha's footprints.
The handles are decorated with
butterflies—an emblem of
joy—and plum blossoms, which
symbolize purity. The knot on
the cover features a relief of
a coiled *li* dragon, holding
its tail in its mouth.

Blue Damask with Peony Design
Qing Dynasty
(A.D. 1644–1911)
Length: 325 cm
Width: 72 cm

This damask features woven peony patterns, using silk thread on a blue ground. The peony symbolizes wealth and rank. This fabric was used exclusively by the rich and the powerful during the Qing Dynasty.

Acknowledgements

In order to organize and present the broad outlines of such an ancient civilization within a limited timeframe, a great deal of cooperation and creativity are necessary. We would like to thank Ambassador Joseph Caron, Ambassador Lu Shumin, Secretary General Mr. Pan Zhenzhou, CMC President and Chief Executive Officer Dr. Victor Rabinovitch, Director of the National Museum of China Mr. Lu Zhangshen, Deputy Director Dr. Dong Qi, Director General of Research and Collections Dr. Stephen Inglis, Director of Ethnology and Cultural Studies Dr. Andrea Laforet, Cultural Counsellor Mr. Zhao Haisheng, Director of the Foreign Affairs Office Mrs. Chen Shujie, Director General of Exhibitions and Programs Ms. Sylvie Morel and First Secretary Li Caiyun for their untiring efforts in completing the exchange agreements and their continuing support for the exhibition itself.

Staff at the National Museum of China deserve particular thanks for their selection and documentation of artifacts and support to the exhibition project: Shao Xiaomeng, An Jiayuan, Chen Chengjun, Chen Yu, Dong Qing, Guan Shuangxi, Han Fulin, Jian Ning, Liu Zhengqing, Shao Yulan, Shan Yueying, Sheng Weiren, Su Qiang, Sun Jian, Sun Jing, Xin Lihua, Wang Liyan, Wang Qiufang, Wang Yi, Wang Yikang, Yang Guimei, Yu Chenglong, Yu Wenrong, Zhang Baohong, Zhang Yan, Zhang Runping and Zhu Min.

Many of my colleagues at the Canadian Museum of Civilization also deserve special thanks: Mark O'Neill, Chantal Amyot, Dario Catana, Susan McLeod O-Reilly, Michèle Courtemanche, Bill Moore, Geoff Wonnacott, Paul Lauzon, Sam Cronk, Brigitte Lafond, Geneviève Eustave, Sylvia Mauro, Deborah Brownrigg, Ginette L. Côté, as well as freelancer Sheila Singhal.

Finally, I would like to acknowledge the assistance of Dr. Michael Knight, Li He and John Stucky of the Asian Art Museum of San Francisco, Dr. Jay Xu of the Art Institute of Chicago, Dr. Jason Sun of the Metropolitan Museum of Art, Amy Poster of the Brooklyn Museum, Dr. Joseph Chang of the Smithsonian Institution's Arthur M. Sackler Gallery of Art, and the East Asian librarians at the University of Toronto, the Royal Ontario Museum, the University of British Columbia, the University of California-Berkeley, and the Harvard-Yenching Library.

To all of you, my profound gratitude and heartfelt thanks.

Ban Seng Hoe
Curator of Asian Studies
Canadian Museum of Civilization